I0798695

The Diane Bish ORGAN BOOK

ARRANGEMENTS BY DIANE BISH

The Diane Bish Organ Book

Christmas Volume 3

Table of Contents

Fred Bock Music Company

to James and Elizabeth King

DRUMMER BOY/PAT-A-PAN

Arranged by Diane Bish

[1]

Sw. Trompette
Ch. Clarinet (or small soft Reed)
Gt. Principal 8′, 4′, Sw. Ch. 8′ to Gt.
Ped. 16′, Ch. to Ped.

OR

[2]

Sw. 8′, 4′, 2
Ch. 8′, 2′
Gt. Principal 8′, 4′, 2′. Mix., Sw. Ch. to Gt.
Ped. Soft 16′, Ch. to Ped.
(Add bright Found. and Mix until full)

* If there are sufficient reeds on the organ, begin with softest and add till full. If not, use registration [2].

+Sw. to Ch.
+4 reed or (Sw. Mix)

+16′ reed or (Sw. to Ch. 4′)
Gt.
+Sw. Ch. to Gt. 4

Gt.
+Gt. scharf
broaden
tr

to Jamie Buswell

O COME, LITTLE CHILDREN

Traditional Carol
Arranged by Diane Bish

Sw. Flutes 8′, 1′
Ch. Flute 8′, Erzahlers
Gt. Flutes 8′, 4′
Ped. 16′, Ch. to Ped.

Andante-light, detached

+Princ. 8, 4, 2
flowing but detached
Gt.
sim.
sim.

8, 4′, 2′, Mix.
Sw.
mf
Sw.
sim.
sim.

Ch. -8′ 2′ Flutes
mp
Ch. 8′ 2′ Flutes
sim.
broaden
p

to Sylvia McNair

O SANCTISSIMA

Sicilian Melody
Arranged by Diane Bish

Sw. Dulce Flute, Celeste
Ch. Strings, Sw. to Ch. 8′, 4′
Gt. Chimes or 8′ Flute
Ped. 16′ Soft, Sw. to Ped.

Gt.
Gt. Chimes
Sw.
-Ch. to Ch. 4
+4 Sw. to Sw.

Ch.
cresc.
Ch.
Strings, - Flutes,- Small principals, 16′, 8′, 4′-Trem.
Ch.
+32′ Bourdon
-16
- Ch. to Ch. 4′
- Sw. to Ch.
rit.
ppp
reduce to quietest strings

to Stacy Blair

CAROLING, CAROLING

Lyric by Wihla Hutson

Music by Alfred Burt
Arranged by Diane Bish

Sw. Found. 8′, 4′, 2′, Mixtures
Ch. Flutes 8′, 4′, 2′
Gt. Principals 8′, 2′
Ped. 16′, Ch. to Ped.

Bright, detached

* The top note may be played alone on the chimes. Otherwise, use suggested registration.

+Sw.
to Ch.
Ch.
Gt.
5
6

Ch.
+Sw.
to Gt.
Gt.
6
+Sw. Reeds 16, 8, 4
fff

to Linda Wood

SILENT NIGHT

Franz Grüber
Arranged by Diane Bish

Sw. Flutes 8′, 4′
Ch. Clarinet, Trem.
Gt. 16′, Sw. to Gt.
Ped. 16′ Gedacht, Sw. to Ped.

a tempo
mf
Gt. Soft 8′ 4′ Fl.
- Erzahler, - Unde maris, 4′ Ch. to Ch., – Flute Celeste
Ch.
mp
sim.

mf

- String
+Celestes, +Sw. to Ch. 8′, 4′
+Ch. Sw. to Gt.
+Ch. to Ch. 16′ With more motion
f a tempo
+Ped. 16′

f

-Ch. to Ch. 16′
-Voix, Celeste
-4′ Fl.
-4′ Sw. to Ch.
8′ Fl. only
ppp

to Anne Martindale Williams

ANGELS WE HAVE HEARD ON HIGH

French Carol
Arranged by Diane Bish

Sw. Flutes 8′, 4′, Princ. 8′, Sw. to Ch.
Ch. Flutes, Strings, Princ. 8′
Gt. Princ. 8′, 2′, Klein Mix.
Ped. 16′, Sw. to Ped.

To Coda
Gt.
ff Full Great

sim.
D.S. al Coda
Ch.
Coda
fff
ffff
+Sw. reeds 16, 8, 4